Published By Nicholas Thompson

@ Edward Mix

Cook at Home: Consider seeking professional guidance to

tailor a low-carb plan to your needs

ISBN 978-87-94477-18-5

TABLE OF CONTENTS

Roasted Pandora Spiced Swordfish Steaks Recipe

INGREDIENTS:

- 1 teaspoon ground cumin

- 1 teaspoon ground coriander

- 1/2 teaspoon ground turmeric

- Salt and black pepper to taste

- Fresh cilantro for garnish

- Lemon wedges for serving

- 4 swordfish steaks (6 ounces each)

- 1 cup plain yogurt

- 2 tablespoons tandoori masala spice blend

- 2 tablespoons lemon juice

- 2 cloves garlic, minced

- 1 tablespoon grated ginger

Directions:

1. Preheat the oven to 425°F (220°C) and line a baking sheet with parchment paper.
2. Combine the yogurt, bandore masala spice blend, lemon juice, minced garlic, grated ginger, ground cumin, ground coriander, ground turmeric, salt, and black pepper in a bowl. Mix well to create a marinade.
3. Place the swordfish steaks in a shallow dish and pour the marinade over them, ensuring they are evenly coated. Let them marinate for at least 15 minutes.
4. Transfer the marinated swordfish steaks to the prepared baking sheet.
5. Roast in the oven for 1012 minutes or until the swordfish is cooked and flakes easily with a fork.

6. Remove from the oven and garnish with fresh cilantro. Serve hot with lemon wedges on the side.

Grilled Cabbage Steaks

Ingredients:

- Bacon (cooked and chopped)

- Ranch dressing

- 1 head of cabbage (thick rounds)

- Kosher salt

- Black pepper powder

- Olive oil

- Scallions (chopped)

- Blue cheese

- Red chili flakes

Directions:

1. Preheat the grill to medium heat.

2. Cut the cabbage head into thick slices, about 1inch thick, to create cabbage steaks.

3. Brush both sides of the cabbage steaks with oil to prevent sticking and promote even grilling.

4. Sprinkle the cabbage steaks with red chili flakes, salt, and black pepper powder to add flavor and a hint of heat.

5. Place the cabbage steaks on the preheated grill and cook for approximately 5 minutes per side, or until they are tender and charred to your desired level.

6. Once grilled, transfer the cabbage steaks to a serving platter.

7. Garnish the grilled cabbage steaks with chopped scallions, crumbled crispy bacon, and crumbled blue cheese. These toppings add a delicious combination of flavors and textures.

8. Drizzle the grilled cabbage steaks with ranch dressing for a creamy and tangy finishing touch.

9. Serve the Grilled Cabbage Steaks hot as a flavorful and unique side dish or even as a vegetarian main course.

Mexican Burrito Zucchini Boats

Ingredients:

- ½ tablespoons of chili powder

- ½ cup of corn

- ½ cup of cherry tomatoes (chopped)

- 3 tablespoons of cilantro (chopped)

- Oil

- ½ teaspoons of cumin powder

- ¼ teaspoons of paprika

- ½ cup of black beans

- 1 cup of cheddar cheese (shredded)

- 1 cup of Monterey Jack cheese (shredded)

- 3 zucchinis (longitudinally sliced)

- 2 tablespoons of olive oil

- 1 lb. of beef (grounded)

- ½ onion (sliced)

- 2 cloves of garlic (diced)

- Kosher salt

- Black pepper powder

Directions:

1. Preheat the oven to 350°F (175°C).

2. Using a spoon, carefully scoop out the insides of the halved zucchinis, creating hollow "boats." Crush the scooped zucchini insides and set them aside.

3. Place the zucchini boats in a baking pan, drizzle them with olive oil, and season with salt and black pepper powder.

4. Bake the zucchini boats in the preheated oven for 10 minutes, or until they are slightly tender.

5. Meanwhile, heat 1 tablespoon of oil in a pan over medium heat.

6. Add diced onion and the crushed zucchini insides to the pan. Sauté until the onion is softened and the zucchini is cooked.

7. Add minced garlic to the pan and sauté for 1 minute, until fragrant.

8. Add ground beef to the pan and cook for about 6 minutes, or until the beef is browned and cooked through.

9. Season the beef mixture with cumin powder, chili powder, paprika, salt, and black pepper powder. Stir well to incorporate the spices.

10. Stir in corn kernels, black beans, and diced tomatoes, and cook for an additional 23 minutes to heat through and allow the flavors to meld together.

11. Remove the zucchini boats from the oven and fill the cavities with the beef filling. Sprinkle both kinds of shredded cheese on top of the filling.

12. Return the filled zucchini boats to the oven and bake for an additional 15 minutes, or until the cheese is melted and bubbly.

13. Garnish the Mexican Burrito Zucchini Boats with chopped cilantro for a fresh and vibrant touch.

14. Serve the zucchini boats hot as a satisfying and flavorful main dish.

15. Mix well until all the ingredients are thoroughly combined and form a doughlike consistency.

16. Transfer the zucchini mixture to the prepared baking pan and press it down to form a crust. Make sure it is evenly spread out.

17. Bake the zucchini crust in the preheated oven for 25 minutes, or until it becomes golden and crispy around the edges.

18. Remove the crust from the oven and spread pizza sauce evenly over the surface of the crust. Add the remaining shredded mozzarella cheese and your desired toppings, such as pepperoni, vegetables, or additional cheese.

19. Return the crust to the oven and bake for an additional 10 minutes, or until the cheese is melted and bubbly.

20. Remove the zucchini pizza crust from the oven and let it cool slightly. Garnish with fresh basil leaves and a sprinkle of red pepper flakes for added flavor and presentation.

21. Slice and serve the Zucchini Pizza Crust as a healthier and lowcarb alternative to traditional pizza crust.

Lebanese Chicken Thighs

Ingredients:

- 30 cloves garlic

- Juice of 2 lemons

- Garlic olive oil as required

- Pepper to taste

- Salt to taste

- 2 Vidalia onion, quartered

- 2 teaspoons dried oregano

- 4 tablespoons ghee

- 4 Roma tomatoes, halved

- 8 chicken thighs

- 1012 baby carrots

Directions:

1. Grease a large cast iron pan with about 34 teaspoons garlic olive oil.
2. Place the chicken thighs on it. Do not overlap the chicken. Leave a little space in between 2 chicken thighs.
3. Place onions, carrots, garlic and tomatoes in between the chicken thighs. Place a few garlic cloves on top of the thighs.
4. Sprinkle lemon juice over the chicken. Sprinkle some more garlic oil over the chicken. Pour melted ghee over it.
5. Sprinkle salt, pepper and oregano.
6. Bake in a preheated oven at 500°F for about 30 minutes.
7. Lower the temperature and bake at 350°F for 20 minutes or the internal temperature of the chicken is 165°F.
8. Broil for a few minutes and cook until crisp.
9. Serve hot.

Snappy Rice Dish

Ingredients:

- 2 tablespoons fresh dill or 2 teaspoons dried dill

- 1 cup broth or water

- 14 ounces chickpeas or kidney beans or pink beans

- Pepper to taste

- 2 cups vegetables, fresh or frozen, cut into bite size pieces

- 2 cups cauliflower, grated to a rice like texture

Directions:

1. Add vegetables and broth into a saucepan and place over medium high heat. Cook until tender.

2. Add rest of the ingredients and heat
    thoroughly.
3. Serve hot.

Tomatoroasted Mackerel

Ingredients:

- 2 tablespoons low fat mayonnaise

- 1 large tomato, sliced

- Pepper to taste

- ½ pound mackerel fillets

- 2 tablespoons fresh basil leaves, chopped

- ¼ teaspoon salt

Directions:

1. Place mackerel on a lined baking sheet. Spread 1tablespoon mayonnaise on each.

2. Place tomato slices and basil on top. Season with salt and pepper.

3. Bake in a preheated oven at 400°F for about 510 minutes or until mackerel turns opaque.

Cinnamon Oatmeal

Ingredients:

- 1 ¾ tsp ground cinnamon

- ½ cup hot water

- 2 Tbsp unsweetened coconut milk

- ½ cup chia seeds

- ½ cup golden flax meal

- ½ cup finely shredded unsweetened coconut

Directions:

1. Combine chia seed, golden flax seed, unsweetened coconut, and cinnamon in an airtight container.

2. Take ½ cup of oatmeal in a serving bowl. Pour ½ cup of water over oatmeal mixture let sit for 35 minutes.

3. Add sweetener and 2 tsp of cream into bowl
    and stir to combine. Top with berries and
    toasted coconut.

Chicken Salad

Ingredients:

- ½ tsp Dijon Mustard

- 1/8 tsp salt

- Black pepper

- 2 cups cubed chicken

- ¼ chopped celery

- ¼ cup mayonnaise

- 2 tbsp sweet relish

- 1 tbsp minced onion

Directions:

1. Combine all ingredients except chicken in large bowl. Mix, and stir in chicken. Cover and refrigerate (optional).

Lemon Dijon Cream Sauce

Ingredients:

- 2 tbs butter

- 1 tbs Dijon

- ½ cup heavy cream

- 1 tbs lemon juice

Directions:

1. Melt butter, add lemon, Dijon and mix the ingredients. Now stir in the heavy cream until a right consistency is formed.

Ketchup

Ingredients:

- 2 pkgs equal

- ½ cup white vinegar

- ½ cup cloves, allspice and cinnamon

- 2 tbs onion powder

- 3 cups canned tomatoes

Directions:

1. Combine all the mentioned ingredients together and simmer the mixture slowly for 1 hour.

2. Now switch off the heat and stir in the sweetener.

3. Cool and pour in a jar. It contains total of 45 carbs. It has a good and different taste in contrast to regular ketchup.

Afghan Peas And Chicken

Ingredients:

- 3 spoons tomato paste

- 1 c. canned green peas

- 1 water

- Salt

- Curry

- Garam masala

- 390 g. chicken breast

- 1 chopped onion

- 1 chopped tomatoes

- 3 garlic cloves

- Turmeric

Directions:

1. To get started on this dish, bring out a pan and place the onion and the oil inside.

2. Allow the onion to fry until it has time to turn a light gold color.

3. At this time you can add in the garlic and then the chopped chicken.

4. Keep on mixing until the chicken as time to become lightly cooked.

5. Place the tomatoes in with this mixture and let it cook for a 1 to 5 minute minutes while you are mixing.

6. Add in the peas and the tomato paste along with a little bit of water to keep it all working.

7. Add in a little bit of salt ot the taste that you like.

8. Garam masala and turmeric are also nice additions.

9. Cover the pan and allow the whole dish to continue cooking until it becomes tender.

Spinach On Egg Toast

Ingredients:

- 5 tbsps. olive oil

- 2 small red onion

- 4 garlic glove

- 360 g baby spinach

- 1 can lowsodium chopped tomatoes

- 5 free range eggs

- Finely chopped fresh dill

- 5 walnut halves

- Salt and pepper

Directions:

1. Heat 1 of the olive oil over medium heat in a mediumsized work.

2. Add the chopped red onion and minced garlic.

3. Stir. Fry until the garlic is fragrant and onion is translucent.

4. Add the chopped spinach and stir to combine.

5. Cook until the spinach has slightly wilted.

6. Add the chopped tomatoes to the pan and stir.

7. Season to taste. Increase heat and let simmer for 5 to 10 more minutes.

8. Remove from heat and transfer to a strainer placed over a bowl for the excess liquid to drain.

9. Add remaining olive oil to a nonstick work over moderate high heat.

10. whisk the eggs until frothy and smooth.

11. Season to taste.

12. Stir in the finely chopped dill and whisk until well combined.

13. Pour the eggs into the wok and let the eggs coat the bottom in an even layer.

14. Let fry until the eggs are nearly set. Flip.

15. Cook for half a minute more. Remove from heat.

16. Place the spinach mixture in the middle of the omelette.

17. Top with crushed walnuts and enjoy immediately!

Ketofriendly Chicken

Ingredients:

- 1/2 cup chopped fresh basil

- 1/4 cup olive oil

- Salt and pepper, to taste

- 1 cup marinara sauce

- 1 cup shredded mozzarella cheese

- 4 boneless, skinless chicken breasts

- 1/2 cup almond flour

- 2 eggs, beaten

- 1/2 cup grated Parmesan cheese

Directions:

1. Preheat the oven to 375°F.

2. Season the chicken breasts with salt and pepper.

3. In a shallow dish, combine the almond flour, grated Parmesan cheese, and chopped basil.

4. Dip the chicken breasts into the beaten eggs, then coat them in the almond flour mixture.

5. Heat the olive oil in a large skillet over mediumhigh heat.

6. Add the chicken breasts and cook for 34 minutes per side, or until golden brown.

7. Remove the chicken from the skillet and place it on a baking sheet.

8. Top each chicken breast with marinara sauce and shredded mozzarella cheese.

9. Bake the chicken in the oven for 1520 minutes, or until the cheese is melted and the chicken is cooked through. Serve and enjoy!

Ketofriendly Pork Tenderloin

Ingredients:

- 1 teaspoon dried rosemary

- Salt and pepper, to taste

- 1/4 cup chicken broth

- 1/4 cup heavy cream

- 1/4 cup grated Parmesan cheese

- 1 lb. pork tenderloin

- 2 tablespoons olive oil

- 2 cloves of garlic, minced

- 1 teaspoon dried thyme

Directions:

1. Preheat the oven to 375°F.
2. Season the pork tenderloin with thyme, rosemary, salt, and pepper.
3. Heat the olive oil in a large skillet over mediumhigh heat.

4. Add the pork tenderloin to the skillet and brown it on all sides.

5. Remove the pork from the skillet and place it on a baking sheet.

6. Bake the pork in the oven for 2530 minutes, or until it reaches an internal temperature of 145°F.

7. Remove the pork from the oven and let it rest for 510 minutes.

8. While the pork is resting, add the garlic to the skillet and sauté for 12 minutes, or until fragrant.

9. Pour in the chicken broth and heavy cream, and bring the mixture to a simmer.

10. Cook for 23 minutes, or until the sauce has thickened stir in the grated Parmesan cheese until it is fully incorporated.

11. Slice the pork tenderloin and serve with the sauce on top.

12. Enjoy your ketofriendly pork tenderloin with a side of your choice.

Oatmeal Made With Almond Milk And Topped With Berries

Ingredients:

- 1/2 cup rolled oats

- 1 cup almond milk

- 1/4 teaspoon ground cinnamon

- 1 tablespoon maple syrup (or to taste)

- 1/4 cup blueberries

- 1/4 cup raspberries

- 1/4 cup slivered almonds

Directions:

1. In a medium saucepan, bring the almond milk to a gentle simmer over medium heat.

2. Once the milk is hot, add the rolled oats and
    stir to combine.

3. Reduce the heat to low and cook for about 10
    minutes, stirring occasionally, until the oats
    are tender.

4. Remove from heat and stir in the cinnamon,
    maple syrup and berries.

5. Serve hot, topped with slivered almonds.
    Enjoy!

Turkey And Cheese Rollups With Cucumber Slices

Ingredients:

- 2 tablespoons of mayonnaise

- 2 tablespoons of Dijon mustard

- Salt and pepper to taste

- 4 slices of delistyle turkey

- 4 slices of cheddar cheese

- 4 slices of cucumber

Directions:

1. Lay out the turkey slices on a cutting board.
2. Spread a layer of mayonnaise and mustard onto each slice of turkey.
3. Lay one slice of cheese onto each slice of turkey, followed by one slice of cucumber.

4. Sprinkle salt and pepper over the top.

5. Starting at one end, roll up each slice of turkey and cheese with the cucumber inside.

6. Secure each rollup with a toothpick.

7. Serve, or refrigerate until ready to enjoy. Enjoy!

Grilled Shrimp With Roasted Vegetables.

Ingredients:

- 2 cloves garlic, minced

- 2 tablespoons olive oil

- 1 teaspoon dried oregano

- 1 teaspoon dried basil

- Salt and pepper to taste

- 1 lb. of large shrimp, peeled and deveined

- 1 red bell pepper, cut into strips

- 1 yellow bell pepper, cut into strips

- 1 orange bell pepper, cut into strips

- 1 red onion, cut into strips

Directions:

1. Preheat the grill to mediumhigh heat.

2. In a large bowl, combine the shrimp, bell peppers, onion, garlic, olive oil, oregano, basil, salt, and pepper.

3. Toss to coat the vegetables and shrimp in the olive oil and seasonings.

4. Place the vegetables and shrimp on the preheated grill.

5. Grill the vegetables and shrimp for about 810 minutes, turning occasionally, until the vegetables are tender and the shrimp are cooked through.

6. Serve the grilled shrimp and vegetables warm. Enjoy!

Turkey And Cheese Rollups

Ingredients:

- 4 slices lowfat cheese (such as Swiss or cheddar)

- 4 pickle spears

- 4 slices turkey breast

Directions:

1. Lay a slice of turkey on a flat surface.
2. Place a slice of cheese on top of the turkey.
3. Roll up a pickle spear inside the turkey and cheese.
4. Secure with a toothpick if needed.
5. Repeat with the remaining ingredients.
6. Serve chilled.

Roasted Edam Me

Ingredients:

- 1 teaspoon soy sauce

- 1/2 teaspoon garlic powder

- Salt and pepper to taste

- 2 cups frozen edamame, thawed

- 1 tablespoon olive oil

Directions:

1. Preheat the oven to 200°C (400°F) and line a baking sheet with parchment paper.

2. In a bowl, toss the edamame with olive oil, soy sauce, garlic powder, salt, and pepper until well coated.

3. Circulate the edamame in a single layer on the baking sheet.

4. Roast for 1520 minutes, stirring once or twice, until crispy.

5. Let cool before serving.

Tuna Cucumber Bites

Ingredients:

- 1 tablespoon chopped fresh dill

- Salt and pepper to taste

- 1 large cucumber, sliced into rounds

- 1 can (5 ounces) tuna, drained

- 2 tablespoons plain Greek yogurt

- 1 tablespoon lemon juice

Directions:

1. In a bowl, mix the tuna, Greek yogurt, lemon juice, dill, salt, and pepper until well combined.
2. Place a spoonful of the tuna mixture on top of each cucumber round.
3. Serve immediately.

Pan Seared Garlic Butter Scallops Recipe

Ingredients:

- 1 tablespoon fresh lemon juice

- 2 tablespoons chopped fresh parsley

- Lemon wedges for serving

- 1 pound large sea scallops

- Salt and black pepper to taste

- 2 tablespoons butter

- 2 cloves garlic, minced

Directions:

1. Pat dry the scallops with a paper towel and season them with salt and black pepper.
2. In a large skillet, melt the butter over mediumhigh heat.

3. Add the scallops to the skillet and cook for 23 minutes on each side until golden brown and opaque in the center.

4. Add the minced garlic to the skillet and cook for 30 seconds until fragrant.

5. Remove the skillet from the heat and drizzle the scallops with fresh lemon juice. Toss them gently to coat.

6. Sprinkle the chopped parsley over the scallops and give them a final toss.

7. Serve hot with lemon wedges on the side.

Sautéed Cajun Shrimp With Garlic And Butter

Recipe

Ingredients:

- 1 tablespoon fresh lemon juice

- 2 tablespoons chopped fresh parsley

- Salt and black pepper to taste

- Lemon wedges for serving

- 1 pound large shrimp, peeled and deveined

- 2 tablespoons Cajun seasoning

- 2 tablespoons butter

- 4 cloves garlic, minced

Directions:

1. In a bowl, season the shrimp with Cajun seasoning, salt, and black pepper. Toss to coat the shrimp evenly.
2. In a large skillet, melt the butter over mediumhigh heat.
3. Add the minced garlic to the skillet and sauté for about 1 minute until fragrant.
4. Add the seasoned shrimp to the skillet and cook on each side for 23 minutes until they turn pink and opaque.
5. Drizzle the fresh lemon juice over the shrimp and toss them gently to coat.
6. Sprinkle the chopped parsley over the shrimp and give them a final toss.
7. Serve hot with lemon wedges on the side.

Shrimp Avocado Basil Salad Lettuce Wraps

Ingredients:

For the Chips

- Black pepper powder

- Kosher salt

- 2 large sweater potatoes (sliced)

For the salad

- Oil

- 1 ½ cups of cherry tomatoes (half sliced)

- 4 leaves of basil (sliced)

- ¾ lb. of shrimps (deveined)

- ¼ onion (chopped)

- 2 avocados (chopped)

- 2 heads of butterhead lettuce

For the marinade

- Kosher salt

- ½ teaspoons paprika

- 3 leaves of basil (sliced)

- 3 tablespoons of olive oil

- Black pepper powder

- 2 cloves of garlic (diced)

- 2 tablespoons of vinegar

- 2 lemons (juice)

Directions:

1. Preheat the oven to 375°F (190°C). Grease a baking pan to prevent sticking.

2. Layer the baking pan with sliced sweet potatoes and sprinkle them with salt and black pepper powder for seasoning.

3. Bake the sweet potatoes for 15 minutes, then flip them and bake for an additional 15 minutes, or until they are tender and golden. Set them aside.

4. In a pan, heat oil over medium heat. Add the shrimps and cook until they turn opaque and the pink color disappears. Remove the cooked shrimps from the pan and set them aside.

5. In a bowl, prepare the marinade by combining minced garlic, vinegar, oil, lemon juice, salt, black pepper powder, paprika, and chopped basil. Mix well to combine the flavors.

6. In another bowl, combine diced tomatoes, diced avocados, sliced red onion, and chopped basil. Mix them gently to avoid smashing the avocado.

7. Add the cooked shrimps and sweet potato chips to the bowl with the salad ingredients. Pour the prepared marinade over the mixture

and toss gently to coat everything with the flavors.

8. Take lettuce leaves and place a generous amount of the shrimp avocado basil salad mixture onto each leaf.

9. Wrap up the lettuce leaves to enclose the filling and serve the Shrimp Avocado Basil Salad Lettuce Wraps.

Low Carb Pot Pies

Ingredients:

- 2 cloves of garlic (diced)

- ½ onion (chopped)

- ½ cup of parmesan cheese (grated)

- 3 large eggs

- 1 carrot (sliced)

- Black pepper powder

- 1 stalk of celery (chopped)

- 1 ½ cups of chicken cubes

- ½ cup of butter

- 2 tablespoons of butter

- 1 large cauliflower (riced and steamed)

- Kosher salt

- 1 cup of chicken broth

- ½ cup of corn

- 1 cup of heavy cream

- 2 tablespoons of plain flour

- Parsley (chopped)

Directions:

1. Preheat the oven to 375°F (190°C).
2. Grease 12 muffin cups with oil or use nonstick cooking spray. Set them aside.
3. In a bowl, combine the riced cauliflower, eggs, grated Parmesan cheese, salt, and pepper. Mix well until all the ingredients are thoroughly combined.
4. Use your fingers to evenly spread the cauliflower mixture along the sides and

bottoms of the greased muffin cups, creating a crust. Press firmly to pack the mixture.

5. Bake the cauliflower crusts in the preheated oven for 15 minutes, or until they are set and slightly golden.

6. While the crusts are baking, heat the butter in a pan over medium heat.

7. Add the celery, onion, carrot, garlic, salt, and pepper to the pan. Sauté for about 3 minutes, until the vegetables are slightly softened.

8. Sprinkle the plain flour over the vegetables and cook for an additional minute, stirring constantly.

9. Slowly pour in the chicken broth and heavy cream, stirring continuously to prevent lumps from forming. Allow the mixture to come to a boil.

10. Once boiling, reduce the heat to simmer and cook for about 3 minutes, until the sauce thickens slightly.

11. Remove the pan from the heat and stir in the cooked chicken, frozen peas, and frozen corn. The filling should be wellcombined.

12. Spoon the chicken mixture into the baked cauliflower crusts, filling them to the top.

13. Return the filled muffin cups to the oven and bake for an additional 9 to 10 minutes, or until the filling is heated through and the tops are golden.

14. Garnish the Low Carb Pot Pies with chopped parsley for added freshness and presentation.

15. Serve the pot pies hot as a delicious and lowcarb alternative to traditional pot pies.

Spaghetti Squash Pizza Nests

Ingredients:

- ½ cup of mini pepperoni

- ⅓ cup of parmesan cheese (grated)

- 2 cups of pizza sauce

- Kosher salt

- 1 teaspoon of garlic powder

- 1 ½ cups of mozzarella cheese (shredded)

- 1 tablespoon of olive oil

- Black pepper powder

- 1 tablespoon of parsley (chopped)

- 1 spaghetti squash (sliced lengthwise)

Directions:

1. Preheat the oven to 400°F (200°C).

2. Place parchment paper on a baking sheet to prevent sticking.

3. Cut the spaghetti squash in half lengthwise and remove the seeds. Drizzle olive oil over the cut sides and sprinkle with salt and black pepper powder.

4. Place the squash halves cutside down on the baking sheet and bake for 45 minutes, or until the flesh is forktender. If using a larger squash, adjust the baking time to 1 hour.

5. Once the squash is cooked, remove it from the oven and let it cool for 10 minutes. Reduce the oven temperature to 375°F (190°C).

6. Using a fork, scrape the flesh of the squash to create spaghettilike strands. Transfer the strands to a bowl.

7. Add garlic powder, grated Parmesan cheese, salt, and black pepper powder to the bowl

with the spaghetti squash strands. Mix well to combine all the ingredients.

8. Grease a muffin pan with a brush to prevent sticking. Take ¼ cup of the spaghetti squash mixture and press it into each muffin cup, forming a nest shape.

9. Bake the spaghetti squash nests in the preheated oven for 15 minutes, or until they are set and slightly golden.

10. Remove the nests from the oven and spoon pizza sauce into each nest.

11. Top the nests with shredded mozzarella cheese and mini pepperoni.

12. Bake the nests for an additional 8 to 10 minutes, or until the cheese is melted and bubbly.

13. Garnish the Spaghetti Squash Pizza Nests with chopped parsley for a fresh and vibrant touch.

14. Serve the nests hot as a fun and lowcarb alternative to traditional pizza.

Cheesy Cauliflower Breadsticks

Ingredients:

- Pepper to taste

- 1 ½ teaspoons dried oregano

- Salt to taste

- 2 eggs, beaten

- 2 cups cauliflower, grated to a rice like texture

- 1 cup mozzarella cheese, shredded + extra to top

- 2 teaspoons, garlic, minced

- ½ teaspoon red pepper flakes or to taste

Directions:

1. Line a baking dish with parchment paper. Set aside.

2. Add cauliflower rice to a microwave safe bowl and cover. Microwave on high for 810 minutes.

3. Transfer into a bowl. Add garlic flakes and red pepper flakes and mix well. Add salt and oregano. Mix well.

4. Add eggs and mozzarella cheese. Mix well.

5. Transfer the mixture into the prepared baking dish. Press well.

6. Bake in a preheated oven at 350°F for 30 minutes.

7. Remove from oven. Sprinkle some more mozzarella cheese.

8. Bake for another 810 minutes or until the cheese melts.

9. Remove from oven and slice. Serve hot.

Keera Curry With Cucumber Raita

Ingredients:

- 1 cup baby spinach

- 2 cloves garlic, chopped

- 1 inch stick cinnamon

- ½ teaspoon cumin seeds, crushed

- ¼ teaspoon crushed dried chili

- ¾ cup low salt beef stock

- Fresh mint leaves to garnish

- 1 pound lean ground beef

- 1 cm fresh ginger, finely chopped

- ½ teaspoon turmeric powder

- ½ teaspoon coriander seeds, crushed

- 9 ounces canned diced tomatoes with its juice

- Pepper to taste

- Salt to taste

- 1 medium onion, finely chopped

For cucumber raita:

- ½ cup plain, high fat yogurt

- 2 teaspoons fresh mint, chopped

- 2 tablespoons cucumber, finely chopped

- Pepper to taste

Directions:

1. Place a skillet over medium heat. Add beef and sauté until brown. Break it simultaneously as it cooks.

2. Add the garlic, ginger, chili, cumin, coriander, cinnamon stick, crushed red chill and pepper and sauté for a couple of minutes. Stir constantly.

3. Add tomatoes and stock and bring to the boil.

4. Cover with a lid and simmer until potatoes and meat are cooked.

5. Add spinach and heat until it wilts. Taste and adjust the seasonings if necessary. Remove from heat.

6. Meanwhile, make cucumber raita as follows: Add all the ingredients of cucumber raita in a bowl. Mix well and refrigerate until use.

7. To serve: Ladle curry into bowls. Garnish with mint leaves and serve with cucumber raita.

Fish With Spicy Green Lentils

Ingredients:

- Pepper to taste

- 1 small onion, chopped

- 1 leek, chopped

- 6 ounces dark green lentils, rinsed, drained

- 1 sprig fresh thyme

- Juice of ½ lemon

- Lemon wedges to serve

- 1 tablespoon extra virgin olive oil

- 1 stalk celery, chopped

- 1 large mild red chili, deseeded, finely chopped

- 1 ½ cups low salt vegetable stalk

- 1 small bay leaf

- A pinch cayenne pepper

- 2 white fish fillets (5 ounces each), skinless

Directions:

1. Place a skillet over medium heat. Add ½ tablespoon oil. When the oil is heated, add onion, celery, chili and leek and sauté for a couple of minutes.

2. Add stock, lentils, thyme and bay leaf and bring to the boil.

3. Reduce heat and cover with a lid. Simmer until tender. If there is liquid remaining in the skillet, then drain the excess liquid.

4. Place fish in a broiler pan with the skin side facing up.

5. Mix together in a bowl, ½ tablespoon oil, and cayenne pepper and lemon juice and brush this mixture over the fish.

6. Sprinkle salt and pepper over it.

7. Broil in a preheated oven until the fish flakes
    when pierced with a fork.

8. To serve: Divide the lentils in 2 serving dishes.
    Place the fish on top and serve garnished with
    lemon wedges.

Chicken & Dumplings

Ingredients:

- ¼ cup frozen peas

- 1 tbsp cornstarch

- 1 ½ Minced garlic

- Pepper

- Seasoned salt

- 2 Boneless, skinless chicken breast

- 2 cups of water

- 2 cans Chicken Broth

- 2 Mission Brand low carb flour soft tortillas

- Onion powder

Directions:

1. In a large pot add water and broth. Add raw chicken breast with garlic, pepper, salt and onion powder.
2. Meanwhile, cut tortilla in half into ½ wide strips. Remove chicken and allow to cool.
3. Bring broth back to boil and add tortilla strips and, shred and add chicken back to broth.
4. With cornstarch and cold water, make a cold curry. Stir into soup. Bring back to a boil, 5 minutes.
5. Lastly, add frozen peas, and allow soup to cool down.

Fake French Toast

Ingredients:

- 4 tbs ricotta

- 2 eggs

- 2 packets splenda

- Nutmeg and cinnamon

Directions:

1. Heat a frying pan and this the mixture of above ingredients into that heated pan.
2. Melt some butter in and keep cooking until it becomes brown.

Ingredients:

- 1 tbs soy flour

- ¼ cup water

- ¼ cup light cream

- 4 oz chopped ham

- 1 tbs Dijon mustard

- 1 tbs butter

Directions:

1. Melt butter and stir in the flour. Put in water, cream and mustard and keep stirring until a thick paste is obtained. Now add ham and serve over crepes.

Ranch Chicken Nuggets

Ingredients:

- 2 lbs. boneless and skinless chicken cut up

- 1 Tbsp. dried parsley

- 1 tsp. dried dill

- 1 tsp. garlic powder

- 1 tsp. onion powder

- 1/ tsp. dried basil

- 1/6 tsp. black pepper

- 1 canned and full fat coconut milk

- 3 fresh egg

- 5 almond flour

Directions:

1. To begin this recipe, turn on the oven and let it heat up to 385 degrees.

2. While the oven is warming up, bring out a bowl and combine together the fresh egg, coconut milk, pepper, basil, onion powder, garlic powder, dill and parsley. Whisk these ingredients together until they are well combined.

3. Next, bring out some kind of storage bag and pour the mixture that you just made into the bag.

4. This is going to be your ranch.

5. Add in the chicken pieces as well. Seal the bag and then shake all of the ingredients around until they are evenly coated.

6. Add in a little bit of the almond flour to the bag and then shake it all around again so that you can get the chicken evenly coated on all sides.

7. Set the bag aside.

8. Brig out a baking sheet and cover it with some parchment paper.

9. Place you covered chicken on top of the baking sheet and then place the baking sheet into the oven.

10. Bake the chicken in the oven for about 30 to 35 minutes.

11. You will know that it is done when the chicken is a golden brown color.

12. Pull the baking pan out of the oven and let the chicken cool down for a 1 to 5 minutes.

Helium Dinner Plate

Ingredients:

- 5 tbsp. butter

- 615 g halloumi cheese

- 5 avocados

- 1 cucumber

- 5 tbsp. olive oil

- 145 ml soured cream

- 5 tbsp. pistachio nuts

- salt and pepper

Directions:

1. Melt butter in a medium frying pan over moderate heat.

2. Fry the halloumi cheese slices on both sides until golden brown, about 1 to 5 minutes on each side.

3. Remove from heat and transfer to plates.

4. Arrange the avocados, pistachios, and cucumber sticks on plates next to the cheese.

5. Spoon in the soured cream.

6. Drizzle the veggies with olive oil.

7. Season with salt and freshly ground black pepper.

Omelet With Superfoods Veggies

Ingredients

- • 1 tsp. olive oilor cumin oil

- 2 cup spinach, cherry tomatoes and 1 spoon of yogurt cheese

- Crushed red pepper flakes and a pinch of dill

5 fresh eggs

• **Salt**

• **Ground black pepper**

Directions:

1. Whisk 5 fresh eggs in a small bowl.
2. Season with salt and ground black pepper and set aside.
3. Heat 2 tsp. olive oil in a medium skillet over medium heat.
4. Add baby spinach, tomatoes, cheese and cook, tossing, until wilted .
5. Add eggs; cook, stirring occasionally, until just set, about 1 to 5 minute.
6. Stir in cheese.
7. Sprinkle with crushed red pepper flakes and dill.

Air Fryer Ratatouille

Ingredients:

- 2 tablespoons olive oil

- 1 teaspoon dried basil

- 1 teaspoon dried oregano

- 1/2 teaspoon dried thyme

- Salt and pepper, to taste

- 1 cup marinara sauce

- 1 eggplant, diced

- 1 zucchini, diced

- 1 yellow squash, diced

- 1 bell pepper, diced

- 1 onion, diced

- 2 cloves garlic, minced

- Chopped fresh parsley, for garnish

Directions:

1. Preheat the air fryer to 400°F (200°C).

2. In a bowl, toss the diced eggplant, zucchini, yellow squash, bell pepper, onion, and minced garlic with olive oil, dried basil, dried oregano, dried thyme, salt, and pepper.

3. Place the seasoned vegetables in the air fryer basket.

4. Cook for 1520 minutes, shaking the basket occasionally, until the vegetables are tender and slightly caramelized.

5. Remove from the air fryer and transfer the vegetables to a serving dish.

6. Pour the marinara sauce over the vegetables and toss gently to combine.

7. Garnish with chopped fresh parsley before serving.

Crispy Garlic Parmesan Air Fryer Green Beans

Ingredients:

- 1/4 cup grated Parmesan cheese

- 1/4 teaspoon garlic powder

- Salt and pepper, to taste

- Lemon wedges, for serving

- 1 pound fresh green beans, trimmed

- 2 tablespoons olive oil

- 2 cloves garlic, minced

Directions:

1. Preheat the air fryer to 400°F (200°C).

2. In a bowl, toss the green beans with olive oil, minced garlic, grated Parmesan cheese, garlic

powder, salt, and pepper until the beans are coated evenly.

3. Place the seasoned green beans in the air fryer basket.

4. Cook for 1012 minutes, shaking the basket occasionally, until the green beans are crispy and slightly charred.

5. Remove from the air fryer and squeeze lemon juice over the beans.

6. Serve hot as a flavorful side dish.

Southwest Stuffed Bell Peppers

Ingredients:

- 1/4 cup chopped fresh cilantro

- 1 tablespoon taco seasoning

- Salt and pepper, to taste

- 1/2 cup shredded cheddar cheese

- Sliced green onions, for garnish

- 4 bell peppers (any color), tops removed and seeds removed

- 1 cup cooked quinoa

- 1 cup black beans, rinsed and drained

- 1 cup corn kernels

- 1/2 cup diced tomatoes

- 1/2 cup diced red onion

Directions:

1. Preheat the air fryer to 375°F (190°C).

2. In a bowl, combine the cooked quinoa, black beans, corn kernels, diced tomatoes, diced red onion, chopped cilantro, taco seasoning, salt, and pepper.

3. Spoon the quinoa mixture into the hollowedout bell peppers, packing them tightly.

4. Place the stuffed bell peppers in the air fryer basket.

5. Cook for 1820 minutes, until the bell peppers are tender and the filling is heated through.

6. Remove from the air fryer and sprinkle the shredded cheddar cheese over the tops of the peppers.

7. Return to the air fryer and cook for an additional 23 minutes, until the cheese is melted and bubbly.

8. Garnish with sliced green onions and serve hot.

Spinach Artichoke Heart Chicken

Ingredients:

- ¼ cup. shredded Parmesan cheese

- ¼ cup. mayonnaise

- 2 tbsp. olive oil

- 2 tbsps. grated mozzarella cheese

- ½ teaspoon. garlic powder

- 4 chicken breasts

- 1 package frozen spinach

- 1 package cream cheese, softened

- ½ can quartered artichoke hearts, drained and chopped

- Salt to taste

Directions:

1. Place the spinach in a bowl and microwave for 2 to 3 minutes. Let chill and drain.

2. Stir in cream cheese, artichoke hearts, Parmesan cheese, mayonnaise, garlic powder, and salt, whisk together. Cut chicken breasts to an even thickness. Spread salt and pepper over chicken breasts per side.

3. Preheat oven to 375 degrees F.

4. In a large skillet over mediumhigh, heat olive oil for 2 to 3 minutes. Lay chicken breasts in a large baking dish, pour spinachartichoke mixture over chicken breasts. Place in the oven and bake at least 165 degrees F.

5. Sprinkle with mozzarella cheese and bake for 1 to 2 minutes more. Serve and enjoy.

Chicken Skewers With Celery Fries

Ingredients:

- 1/4 chicken broth

- For the fries

- 1 lb celery root

- 2 tbsp olive oil

- ½ tsp salt

- 2 chicken breasts

- ½ tsp salt

- ¼ tsp ground black pepper

- 2 tbsp olive oil

- ¼ tsp ground black pepper

Directions:

1. Set an oven to 400ºF. Grease and line a baking
   sheet. In a large bowl, mix oil, spices and the

chicken; set in the fridge for 10 minutes while covered.

2. Peel and chop celery root to form fry shapes and place into a separate bowl.

3. Apply oil to coat and add pepper and salt for seasoning. Arrange to the baking tray in an even layer and bake for 10 minutes.

4. Take the chicken from the refrigerator and thread onto the skewers.

5. Place over the celery, pour in the chicken broth, then set in the oven for 30 minutes. Serve with lemon wedges.

Ketofriendly Cheese

Ingredients:

- 1/4 teaspoon paprika

- 1/4 teaspoon garlic powder

- 1 egg, beaten

- 1 cup shredded cheddar cheese

- 2 tablespoons almond flour

- 1/4 teaspoon salt

Directions:

1. Preheat the oven to 350°F.
2. In a mixing bowl, combine the shredded cheddar cheese, almond flour, salt, paprika, and garlic powder.
3. Mix in the beaten egg until a dough forms.

4. Roll the dough out between two pieces of parchment paper to a thickness of 1/8 inch.

5. Use a pizza cutter or knife to cut the dough into small crackersized squares.

6. Place the crackers on a baking sheet lined with parchment paper.

7. Bake in the oven for 1012 minutes, or until the crackers are golden brown and crispy.

8. Remove from the oven and let cool on the baking sheet for a few minutes.

9. Serve and enjoy!

Keto friendly Deviled Eggs

Ingredients:

- 6 large eggs

- 2 tablespoons mayonnaise

- 1 tablespoon Dijon mustard

- 1/2 teaspoon paprika

- Salt and pepper, to taste

- 2 tablespoons chopped fresh chives

Directions:

1. Place the eggs in a pot and cover them with cold water.

2. Bring the water to a boil, then turn off the heat and let the eggs sit in the hot water for 12 minutes.

3. Remove the eggs from the water and place them in a bowl of ice water to cool.

4. Peel the eggs and cut them in half lengthwise.

5. Remove the yolks and place them in a mixing bowl.

6. Mash the yolks with a fork and mix in the mayonnaise, Dijon mustard, paprika, salt, and pepper.

7. Spoon the yolk mixture back into the egg whites.

8. Garnish with chopped chives.

9. Serve and enjoy!

Keto Egg Muffins:

Ingredients:

- ¼ cup of diced bell pepper

- ¼ cup of shredded cheese

- Salt and pepper to taste

- 4 eggs

- ½ cup of cooked spinach

- ¼ cup of diced onion

Directions:

1. Preheat oven to 350°F and spray a 12cup muffin tin with nonstick cooking spray.

2. In a medium bowl, whisk together eggs, spinach, onion, bell pepper, cheese, salt, and pepper.

3. Divide the mixture evenly into the 12 muffin cups.

4. Bake for 20 minutes or until muffin tops are golden brown and eggs are cooked through.

5. Enjoy warm or cool and store in an airtight container in the refrigerator for up to four days.

Avocado Toast:

Ingredients:

- 2 teaspoons of olive oil

- Salt and pepper to taste

- 1 ripe avocado

- 2 slices of whole grain bread

Directions:

1. Toast the bread.
2. Use a fork to mash the avocado in a small bowl.
3. Spread the mashed avocado onto the toasted bread.
4. Drizzle with olive oil and sprinkle with salt and pepper.
5. Enjoy immediately.

Baked Egg Cups:

Ingredients:

- ¼ cup of shredded cheese

- Salt and pepper to taste

- 4 eggs

- ¼ cup of diced ham

- ¼ cup of diced bell pepper

Directions:

1. Preheat oven to 350°F and spray a 12cup muffin tin with nonstick cooking spray.
2. Divide the ham, bell pepper, and cheese evenly into the 12 muffin cups.
3. Add one cracked egg to each muffin cup.
4. Bake for 20 minutes or until egg whites are cooked through.

5. Sprinkle with salt and pepper and enjoy
    warm.

Tomato and Mozzarella Skewers

Ingredients:

- Fresh basil leaves

- Balsamic glaze for drizzling

- 8 cherry tomatoes

- 8 small fresh mozzarella balls

Directions:

1. Thread a cherry tomato, mozzarella ball, and basil leaf onto each skewer.
2. Drizzle with balsamic glaze.
3. Serve chilled.

Almond and Berry Smoothie

Ingredients:

- 1/2 teaspoon honey (optional)

- Ice cubes (optional)

- 1 cup unsweetened almond milk

- 1/2 cup mixed berries (such as strawberries, raspberries, blueberries)

- 1 tablespoon almond butter

Directions:

1. In a blender, combine the almond milk, mixed berries, almond butter, honey, and ice cubes (if desired).
2. Blend until smooth and creamy.
3. Pour into a glass and serve.

Pan seared Pandora Spiced Salmon Recipe

97

Ingredients:

- 1 teaspoon ground coriander

- 1/2 teaspoon ground turmeric

- Salt and black pepper to taste

- Fresh cilantro for garnish

- Lemon wedges for serving

- 4 salmon fillets (6 ounces each)

- 2 tablespoons tandoori masala spice blend

- 2 tablespoons plain yogurt

- 1 tablespoon lemon juice

- 1 teaspoon ground cumin

Directions:

1. Combine the tandoori masala spice blend, plain yogurt, lemon juice, ground cumin, coriander, turmeric, salt, and black pepper in a bowl. Mix well to create a marinade.

2. Pat dry the salmon fillets with a paper towel and rub them with the marinade, ensuring they are evenly coated. Let them marinate for at least 10 minutes.

3. Heat a large skillet over mediumhigh heat and add a drizzle of oil.

4. Place the marinated salmon fillets in the skillet, skinside down, and sear for 45 minutes. Flip the fillets and roast for 34 minutes or until the salmon is cooked to your desired level of doneness.

5. Remove from the heat and garnish with fresh cilantro.

6. Serve hot with lemon wedges on the side.

Spicy Sautéed Garlic Butter Lobster Tails Recipe

Ingredients:

- 1 teaspoon red pepper flakes

- 1 tablespoon chopped fresh parsley

- Salt and black pepper to taste

- Lemon wedges for serving

- 2 lobster tails

- 4 tablespoons butter

- 4 cloves garlic, minced

Directions:

1. Using kitchen shears, carefully cut through the top shell of each lobster tail, stopping before reaching the tail fan.

2. Gently lift the meat from the shell, keeping it attached at the tail end.

3. Melt the butter in a large skillet over mediumhigh heat.

4. Add the minced garlic and red pepper flakes to the skillet and sauté for about 1 minute, until fragrant.

5. Place the lobster tails in the skillet, fleshside down, and cook for 45 minutes until the meat is opaque and slightly firm.

6. Flip the lobster tails and cook for 34 minutes.

7. Remove from the heat and sprinkle with fresh parsley—season with salt and black pepper to taste.

8. Serve hot with lemon wedges on the side.

Panfried Moroccan Spiced Fish With Couscous Recipe

Ingredients:

- 2 tablespoons olive oil

- 1 cup couscous

- 1 1/2 cups vegetable broth or water

- 1/4 cup raisins

- 1/4 cup chopped fresh parsley

- Lemon wedges for serving

- 4 fish fillets (such as cod, tilapia, or halibut)

- 2 teaspoons ground cumin and 2 teaspoon ground coriander

- 1 teaspoon ground paprika

- 1/2 teaspoon ground turmeric and ½ teaspoon ground cinnamon

- Salt and black pepper to taste

Directions:

1. In a small bowl, combine the ground cumin, coriander, paprika, turmeric, cinnamon, salt, and black pepper.

2. Season the fish fillets with the spice mixture, ensuring they are evenly coated.

3. Heat the olive oil in a large skillet over medium heat.

4. Add the fish fillets to the skillet and cook for 34 minutes on each side until golden brown and cooked through.

5. Bring the vegetable oil or water can. Add the couscous and raisins, then remove from heat. Let it sit for about 5 minutes until the couscous absorbs the liquid.

6. Fluff the couscous with a fork and stir in the chopped parsley.

7. Serve the panfried fish fillets on a bed of couscous. Garnish with fresh parsley and serve with lemon wedges on the side.

Zucchini Ravioli

Ingredients:

- Kosher salt

- 4 large zucchinis

- ¼ cup of basil (sliced)

- 2 cups of marinara sauce

- 1 clove of garlic (diced)

- Black pepper powder

- 1 egg

- 2 cups of ricotta cheese

- ½ cup of Parmesan cheese (grated)

- ½ cup of mozzarella cheese

- 1 tablespoon of olive oil

Directions:

1. Preheat the oven to 375°F (190°C). Grease a baking pan to prevent sticking.

2. Prepare the zucchini noodles by cutting off both ends of the zucchinis and slicing them into thin strips. Repeat this process for all the zucchinis.

3. In a bowl, beat the egg. Add 2 tablespoons of chopped basil, ricotta cheese, minced garlic, grated Parmesan cheese, salt, and pepper. Mix all the filling ingredients together until well combined.

4. Lay the zucchini strips lengthwise on a chopping board, slightly overlapping each other. Place 2 more zucchini strips perpendicularly at the center of the previous strips, creating a cross shape.

5. Spoon 1 teaspoon of the filling mixture onto the center of the crossshaped zucchini strips.

6. Fold the zucchini strips over the filling, covering it completely. Repeat this process with the remaining zucchini strips to create the zucchini ravioli.

7. Place the zucchini ravioli in the greased baking pan with the folded side facing down.

8. Spread marinara sauce over the top of the zucchini ravioli, ensuring they are well coated. Sprinkle shredded mozzarella cheese over the marinara sauce.

9. Bake the zucchini ravioli in the preheated oven for 25 to 30 minutes, or until the cheese is melted and bubbly.

10. Garnish the Zucchini Ravioli with grated Parmesan cheese and additional chopped basil.

11. Serve the ravioli hot, either on its own or with a side salad.

Sub Keto Rollups

Ingredients:

- 1 clove of garlic (grated)

- 1 tablespoon of olive oil

- 6 slices of ham

- 12 slices of pepperoni

- ½ cup of red peppers (shredded)

- 1 cup of romaine lettuce (shredded)

- 2 tablespoons of vinegar

- ½ cup of mayonnaise

- 6 slices of provolone cheese

- 12 slices of salami

- 1 teaspoon of Italian seasoning

Directions:

1. In a bowl, whisk together minced garlic, oil, Italian seasoning, mayonnaise, and vinegar to prepare the Italian dressing.

2. To assemble each rollup, place 2 slices of salami on a flat surface, slightly overlapping them. Top with a slice of provolone cheese, a slice of ham, and two slices of pepperoni.

3. Add a small amount of romaine lettuce leaves and roasted peppers in the center of the stack of meats and cheeses.

4. Drizzle the Italian dressing over the filling ingredients.

5. Carefully roll up the ingredients tightly, starting from one end. Repeat the procedure to make a total of 6 rollups.

6. Serve the Sub Keto RollUps as a delicious and lowcarb alternative to traditional sandwiches.

Refreshing Lowcarb Chocolate Mousse

Ingredients:

- 3 tsp vanilla extract

- 28 g cocoa powder

- 1450 ml coconut milk

Directions:

1. Place the coconut milk cans in the fridge and let sit overnight.
2. Refrigeration separates the milk into coconut water and solid cream.
3. Use a fine drainer to separate the solid coconut cream from the water.
4. Set the coconut cream aside in a mixing bowl.
5. Add vanilla extract and cocoa powder to the coconut cream bowl.
6. Use a handheld mixer to whisk the ingredients until well combined.

7. Place an equal amount of the mixture into 8 serving bowls.

8. Decorate with fresh mint leaves or 810 fresh raspberries.

Zucchini Spaghetti With Turkey Bolognese Sauce

Ingredients:

- 3 tbsp pesto sauce

- 1 cup diced onion

- 2 cups broccoli florets

- 6 cups zucchini, spiralized

- 2 cups sliced mushrooms

- 2 tsp olive oil

- 1 pound ground turkey

Directions:

1. Heat the oil in a skillet. Add zucchini and cook for 23 minutes, stirring continuously; set aside.

2. Add turkey to the skillet and cook until browned, about 78 minutes. Transfer to a

plate. Add onion and cook until translucent, about 3 minutes.

3. Add broccoli and mushrooms, and cook for 7 more minutes. Return the turkey to the skillet. Stir in the pesto sauce.

4. Cover the pan, lower the heat, and simmer for 15 minutes. Stir in zucchini pasta and serve immediately.

Stuffed Avocados With Chicken

Ingredients:

- ½ tsp onion powder

- ½ tsp garlic powder

- 1 tsp paprika

- Salt and black pepper, to taste

- 2 tbsp lemon juice

- 2 avocados, cut in half and pitted

- ¼ cup pesto

- 1 tsp dried thyme

- 2 tbsp cream cheese

- 1½ cups chicken, cooked and shredded

- Salt and ground black pepper, to taste

- ¼ tsp cayenne pepper

Directions:

1. Scoop the insides of the avocado halves, and place the flesh in a bowl. Add in the chicken.
2. Stir in the remaining ingredients. Stuff the avocado cups with chicken mixture and enjoy.

Garlic Herb Air Fryer Mushrooms

Ingredients:

- 1 tablespoon chopped fresh parsley

- 1 teaspoon dried thyme

- 1/2 teaspoon dried rosemary

- Salt and pepper, to taste

- 1 pound button mushrooms, cleaned and stems trimmed

- 2 tablespoons olive oil

- 2 cloves garlic, minced

Directions:

1. Preheat the air fryer to 375°F (190°C).
2. In a bowl, toss the mushrooms with olive oil, minced garlic, chopped fresh parsley, dried thyme, dried rosemary, salt, and pepper.

3. Place the seasoned mushrooms in the air fryer
    basket.

4. Cook for 1012 minutes, shaking the basket
    occasionally, until the mushrooms are tender
    and slightly browned.

5. Remove from the air fryer and serve hot as a
    flavorful side dish or topping.

Bang Shrimp

Ingredients:

- 1 tablespoon Sriracha sauce

- 1 tablespoon honey

- Juice of 1/2 lime

- Salt and pepper, to taste

- Chopped fresh cilantro, for garnish

- 1 pound shrimp, peeled and deveined

- 1/2 cup plain Greek yogurt

- 2 tablespoons mayonnaise

- 1 tablespoon sweet chili sauce

Directions:

1. Preheat the air fryer to 400°F (200°C).

2. In a bowl, whisk together the Greek yogurt,
    mayonnaise, sweet chili sauce, Sriracha sauce,
    honey, lime juice, salt, and pepper to make
    the bang bang sauce.
3. Coat the shrimp in the bang bang sauce,
    making sure they are evenly coated.
4. Place the coated shrimp in the air fryer
    basket.
5. Cook for 68 minutes, shaking the basket
    halfway through cooking, until the shrimp are
    pink and cooked through.
6. Remove from the air fryer and garnish with
    chopped fresh cilantro.
7. Serve hot as a delicious appetizer or main
    dish.

Sesame Soy Air Fryer Brussels Sprouts

Ingredients:

- 1 teaspoon minced garlic

- 1 tablespoon sesame seeds

- Salt and pepper, to taste

- Sliced green onions, for garnish

- 1 pound Brussels sprouts, halved

- 2 tablespoons lowsodium soy sauce

- 1 tablespoon sesame oil

- 1 tablespoon honey

- 1 teaspoon grated ginger

Directions:

1. Preheat the air fryer to 400°F (200°C).

2. In a bowl, whisk together the soy sauce, sesame oil, honey, grated ginger, minced garlic, sesame seeds, salt, and pepper.

3. Toss the halved Brussels sprouts in the soy sauce mixture until coated evenly.

4. Place the Brussels sprouts in the air fryer basket.

5. Cook for 1215 minutes, shaking the basket occasionally, until the Brussels sprouts are crispy and caramelized.

6. Remove from the air fryer and garnish with sliced green onions before serving.

Cajun Air Fryer Catfish

Ingredients:

- 2 tablespoons olive oil

- Lemon wedges, for serving

- Chopped fresh parsley, for garnish

- 4 catfish fillets

- 2 tablespoons Cajun seasoning

- 1/4 cup cornmeal

Directions:

1. Preheat the air fryer to 400°F (200°C).

2. Season the catfish fillets with Cajun seasoning, ensuring they are coated evenly.

3. In a shallow dish, combine the cornmeal and olive oil to form a paste.

4. Dip each seasoned catfish fillet into the cornmeal mixture, pressing lightly to adhere.

5. Place the coated catfish fillets in the air fryer basket.

6. Cook for 1012 minutes, flipping the fillets halfway through cooking, until the fish is cooked through and crispy.

7. Remove from the air fryer and squeeze lemon juice over the fillets.

8. Garnish with chopped fresh parsley and serve hot.

Teriyaki Vegetable Stir Fry

Ingredients:

- 1 tablespoon rice vinegar

- 1 tablespoon honey or maple syrup

- 1 teaspoon grated ginger

- 2 cloves garlic, minced

- 1 tablespoon cornstarch

- 1 tablespoon water

- Sesame seeds, for garnish

- 2 cups mixed vegetables (such as bell peppers, broccoli, carrots, snap peas)

- 2 tablespoons lowsodium soy sauce

- 2 tablespoons teriyaki sauce

- Sliced green onions, for garnish

Directions:

1. Preheat the air fryer to 400°F (200°C).

2. In a small bowl, whisk together the soy sauce, teriyaki sauce, rice vinegar, honey or maple syrup, grated ginger, and minced garlic to make the sauce.

3. In another small bowl, mix the cornstarch and water to create a slurry.

4. Place the mixed vegetables in the air fryer basket.

5. Pour the teriyaki sauce over the vegetables and toss to coat evenly.

6. Cook for 810 minutes, shaking the basket occasionally, until the vegetables are tendercrisp.

7. Pour the cornstarch slurry over the cooked vegetables and toss to coat, allowing the sauce to thicken.

8. Garnish with sesame seeds and sliced green onions before serving.

Honey Lime Air Fryer Chicken Wings

Ingredients:

- 1 tablespoon lime juice

- 1 teaspoon lime zest

- 1 teaspoon garlic powder

- Salt and pepper, to taste

- 1 pound chicken wings

- 2 tablespoons honey

- 2 tablespoons soy sauce

- Chopped fresh cilantro, for garnish

Directions:

1. Preheat the air fryer to 400°F (200°C).

2. In a bowl, combine the honey, soy sauce, lime
    juice, lime zest, garlic powder, salt, and
    pepper to make the marinade.

3. Add the chicken wings to the marinade and
    toss to coat them thoroughly.

4. Place the chicken wings in the air fryer basket.

5. Cook for 2025 minutes, flipping the wings
    halfway through cooking, until the chicken is
    cooked through and crispy.

6. Remove from the air fryer and let cool for a
    few minutes.

7. Garnish with chopped fresh cilantro and serve
    hot.

Herby Chicken Meatballs

Ingredients:

- ¼ cup mozzarella cheese, grated

- 1 tbsp dry Italian seasoning

- ¼ cup hot sauce + more for serving

- 1 egg

- 1 pound ground chicken

- Salt and black pepper, to taste

- 2 tbsp ranch dressing

- ½ cup almond flour

Directions:

1. Using a bowl, combine chicken meat, pepper, ranch dressing, Italian seasoning, flour, hot sauce, mozzarella cheese, salt, and the egg.

2. Form 9 meatballs, arrange them on a lined

    baking tray and cook for 16 minutes at 480ºF.

3. Place the chicken meatballs in a bowl and

    serve along with hot sauce.

Chicken, Broccoli & Cashew Stirfry

Ingredients:

- 2 tsp xanthan gum

- 1 lemon, juiced

- 1 cup unsalted cashew nuts

- 2 cups broccoli florets

- 1 white onion, thinly sliced

- Pepper to taste

- 2 chicken breasts, cut into strips

- 3 tbsp olive oil

- 2 tbsp soy sauce

- 2 tsp white wine vinegar

- 1 tsp erythritol

Directions:

1. In a bowl, mix the soy sauce, vinegar, lemon juice, erythritol, and xanthan gum. Set aside.
2. Heat the oil in a wok and fry the cashew for 4 minutes until goldenbrown. Remove the cashews into a paper towel lined plate and set aside.
3. Sauté the onion in the same oil for 4 minutes until soft and browned; add to the cashew nuts.
4. Add the chicken to the wok and cook for 4 minutes; include the broccoli and pepper.
5. Stirfry and pour the soy sauce mixture in. Stir and cook the sauce for 4 minutes and pour in the cashews and onion. Stir once more, cook for 1 minute, and turn the heat off.
6. Serve the chicken stirfry with some steamed cauli rice.

Chicken Breasts With Walnut Crust

Ingredients:

- 3 tbsp coconut oil

- 1½ cups walnuts, ground

- 4 chicken breast halves, boneless and skinless

- 1 egg, whisked

- Salt and black pepper, to taste

Directions:

1. Using a bowl, add in walnuts and the whisked egg in another.
2. Season the chicken, dip in the egg and then in pecans. Warm oil in a pan over mediumhigh heat and brown the chicken.
3. Remove the chicken pieces to a baking sheet, set in the oven, and bake for 10 minutes at 350º F. Serve topped with lemon slices.

Baked Salmon With Broccoli And Cauliflower

INGREDIENTS:

- 1/2 cup chicken broth

- 2 tablespoons lemon juice

- 2 tablespoons butter

- 2 tablespoons chopped fresh parsley

- 4 (6-ounce) salmon fillets

- 2 tablespoons olive oil

- Salt and pepper to taste

- 2 cups broccoli florets

- 2 cups cauliflower florets

Directions:

1. Set the oven to 375 degrees Fahrenheit.

2. Place the salmon fillets on a baking sheet and brush with the olive oil. Season with salt and pepper.

3. In a separate baking dish, combine the broccoli and cauliflower. Pour the chicken broth and lemon juice over the vegetables and dot with butter.

4. Bake both the salmon and vegetables for 15 minutes.

5. Sprinkle the parsley over the salmon and vegetables and bake for an additional 10 minutes.

6. Serve the salmon with the broccoli and cauliflower. Enjoy!

Chicken Pram Stuffed Bell Peppers

Ingredients:

- 3 cloves of garlic (diced)

- 1 ½ cups of marinara sauce

- Black pepper powder

- 4 bell peppers (longitudinally halved)

- 1 tablespoon of parsley (chopped)

- 3 cups of mozzarella cheese (shredded)

- Red chili flakes

- Kosher salt

- 12 oz. of frozen bread chicken (cooked)

- ½ cup of chicken broth

- ½ cup of parmesan cheese, plus for garnishing, (grated)

Directions:

1. Preheat the oven to 400°F (200°C).

2. In a bowl, combine marinara sauce, red chili flakes, black pepper powder, salt, minced garlic, chopped parsley, 2 cups of shredded mozzarella cheese, grated Parmesan cheese, and cooked chicken. Mix well until all the ingredients are thoroughly combined.

3. Cut the bell peppers in half lengthwise and remove the seeds and membranes to create cavities for stuffing.

4. Fill each bell pepper half with the chicken mixture, distributing it evenly among the peppers. Sprinkle the remaining shredded mozzarella cheese on top of the stuffed peppers.

5. Take a baking pan and pour in enough chicken broth to cover the bottom of the pan.

6. Place the stuffed bell peppers in the pan with the broth. Cover the pan with aluminum foil.

7. Bake the stuffed bell peppers in the
   preheated oven for 1 hour, or until the
   peppers are tender and the filling is heated
   through.

8. Remove the foil and broil the stuffed peppers
   for 1 minute, or until the cheese on top
   becomes golden and bubbly.

9. Serve the Chicken Parm Stuffed Bell Peppers
   hot, garnished with fresh parsley and grated
   Parmesan cheese for added flavor and
   presentation.

Zucchini Pizza Crust

Ingredients:

- Basil leaves

- ½ cup of parmesan cheese (grated)

- ¼ cup of pepperoni

- ¼ cup of cornstarch

- 2 cloves of garlic (diced)

- ½ teaspoons oregano (dried)

- Black pepper powder

- 3 zucchinis (grated)

- 3 cups of mozzarella cheese (shredded)

- ¼ cup of pizza sauce

- 1 egg

- Kosher salt

- Red pepper flakes

Directions:

1. Preheat the oven to 425°F (220°C).
2. Place parchment paper on a baking pan to prevent sticking.
3. Grate the zucchinis and remove excess moisture by using a cheesecloth or a clean kitchen towel. Squeeze the grated zucchinis to remove as much liquid as possible.

Greek Yogurt With Berries And Almond Slivers

INGREDIENTS:

- 1 cup Greek yogurt

- 1/2 cup fresh berries (blackberries, raspberries, blueberries, etc.)

- 2 tablespoons almond slivers

- 1 teaspoon honey (optional)

Directions:

1. Greek yogurt should be put in a bowl.

2. Add the fresh berries, almond slivers, and honey (if using) to the bowl.

3. Stir the INGREDIENTS: together until everything is evenly distributed.

4. Serve chilled and enjoy!

Tuna Salad With Lettuce, Tomatoes, And A Lowcarb Dressing

INGREDIENTS:

- 3 tablespoons white wine vinegar

- 1 teaspoon dried oregano

- 1 teaspoon garlic powder

- Salt and pepper to taste

- 2 cans tuna, drained

- 3 cups of lettuce, shredded

- 2 tomatoes, diced

- 1/3 cup olive oil

Directions:

1. In a large bowl, combine the tuna, lettuce, and tomatoes.

2. In a small bowl, whisk together the olive oil, white wine vinegar, oregano, garlic powder, salt, and pepper.

3. Pour the dressing over the tuna salad, and toss to combine.

4. Serve immediately, or chill in the refrigerator until ready to serve. Enjoy!

Cajun Baked Tilapia With Vegetables Recipe

INGREDIENTS:

- 1/2 teaspoon garlic powder, 1/2 teaspoon onion powder and 1/2 teaspoon dried thyme

- Salt and black pepper to taste

- 2 tablespoons olive oil

- 2 cups mixed vegetables (such as bell peppers, zucchini, and cherry tomatoes), chopped

- Fresh parsley for garnish and lemon wedges for serving

- 4 tilapia fillets

- 1 tablespoon Cajun seasoning

- 1 teaspoon paprika

Directions:

1. Preheat the oven to 400°F (200°C) and line a baking sheet with parchment paper.

2. Combine the Cajun seasoning, paprika, garlic powder, onion powder, dried thyme, salt, and black pepper in a small bowl.

3. Rub the spice mixture onto both sides of the tilapia fillets and place them on the prepared baking sheet.

4. Toss the mixed vegetables with olive oil, salt, and black pepper in a separate bowl.

5. Arrange the seasoned vegetables around the tilapia fillets on the baking sheet.

6. Bake in the preheated oven for about 1520 minutes or until the tilapia is cooked through and the vegetables are tender.

7. Garnish with fresh parsley and serve hot with lemon wedges on the side.

Baked Spiced Coconut Curry Mussels Recipe

INGREDIENTS:

- 1 tablespoon fish sauce

- 1 tablespoon lime juice

- 1 tablespoon brown sugar

- 2 cloves garlic, minced

- 1 thumbsized piece of ginger, grated

- 1 stalk lemongrass, bruised

- 2 pounds fresh mussels, cleaned and debearded

- 1 can (14 ounces) of coconut milk

- 2 tablespoons red curry paste

- Fresh cilantro for garnish

- Lime wedges for serving

Directions:

1. Preheat the oven to 425°F (220°C).

2. Combine the coconut milk, red curry paste, fish sauce, lime juice, brown sugar, minced garlic, grated ginger, and lemongrass in a large baking dish.

3. Add the cleaned mussels to the baking dish and toss to coat them in the coconut curry mixture.

4. Cover the baking dish with foil and bake in the oven for about 1215 minutes or until the mussels have opened.

5. Remove from the oven and discard any mussels that did not open.

6. Garnish with fresh cilantro and serve hot with lime wedges on the side.